Seeking Your Face

Seeking God's Face

Learning to walk with God in prayer

Beryl Adamsbaum

Text copyright © Beryl Adamsbaum 2003, 2004
The author asserts the moral right
to be identified as the author of this work

Published by
The Bible Reading Fellowship
First Floor, Elsfield Hall
15–17 Elsfield Way, Oxford OX2 8FG

ISBN 1 84101 370 6
Original edition published in English under the title *Seeking God's Face—
Learning to Walk with God in Prayer* by Opine Publishing, Maryland, USA.
Copyright © Opine Publishing 2003

UK edition first published 2004
1 3 5 7 9 10 8 6 4 2 0
All rights reserved

Acknowledgments
Unless otherwise stated, scripture quotations are taken from the *Holy Bible,
New International Version*, copyright © 1973, 1978, 1984 by International
Bible Society, are used by permission of Hodder & Stoughton Limited. All
rights reserved. 'NIV' is a registered trademark of International Bible Society.
UK trademark number 1448790.

Scripture quotations taken from The New Revised Standard Version of the
Bible, Anglicized Edition, copyright © 1989, 1995 by the Division of
Christian Education of the National Council of the Churches of Christ in the
USA, and are used by permission. All rights reserved.

Scriptures quoted from the Good News Bible published by The Bible
Societies/HarperCollins Publishers Ltd, UK © American Bible Society 1966,
1971, 1976, 1992, used with permission.

Extracts from the Authorized Version of the Bible (The King James Bible), the
rights in which are vested in the Crown, are reproduced by permission of the
Crown's patentee, Cambridge University Press.

The Living Bible copyright © 1971 by Tyndale House Publishers.

The Holy Bible, New King James Version. Copyright © 1982 by Thomas
Nelson, Inc.

Scripture quotations from THE MESSAGE. Copyright © by Eugene H. Peterson
1993, 1994, 1995. Used by permission of NavPress Publishing Group.

A catalogue record for this book is available from the British Library

Printed and bound in Great Britain by
Bookmarque, Croydon

CONTENTS

Introduction

The Seeking Heart

Hear, O Lord, when I cry with my voice! Have mercy also upon me, and answer me. When You said, 'Seek My face', my heart said to You, 'Your face, Lord, I shall seek.'

PSALM 27:7–8 (NJKV)

My first thought when considering this book on prayer was, 'Where do I start?' Following closely on from that was, 'Where do I stop?' Prayer is a vast, multi-faceted subject that encompasses the whole of life.

As my relationship with God has deepened, and as I am learning to draw closer to him, I want to share aspects of prayer that will cause you a tremor of joy and anticipation similar to that which I have experienced in his presence.

I trust that this little book will cause a yearning for God to rise up within you, a hunger and thirst for him that can be assuaged only as you come to him, feed on his word, and seek his face in prayer.

In Psalm 27:7 and 8, the psalmist expresses his deep longing to communicate with God. He yearns to know that God has heard his call for help and will answer. He cries out, as one would expect, with his voice: 'Hear, O Lord, when I cry with my voice!'

However, as C.H. Spurgeon pointed out in *The Treasury of David*, in the next sentence the psalmist's heart speaks: '...my heart said to You, "Your face, Lord, I shall seek."' Spurgeon believed this signified a firm intention, a deep desire, and a solemn resolve to seek God's face.[1]

In his *Commentary on the Psalms*, E.W. Hengstenberg points out that to seek the face of someone means to 'seek to be admitted to his presence'. Hengstenberg makes a comparison with the expression to 'seek an audience with a ruler' (Proverbs 29:26), and explains that only those who enjoy the favour of the ruler are admitted into his presence. Similarly, 'to seek the face of the Lord is to seek to be admitted into his presence', and so in reality 'to enjoy his favour'.[2]

Note in Psalm 27 that it is God who takes the initiative. God wants to open himself up to the psalmist and make himself known to him. It is thrilling to me to realize that it is still God's desire to reveal himself to his children today!

Will you accept his invitation to seek his face? 'You will seek me and find me when you seek me with all your heart,' says God (Jeremiah 29:13).

How do we seek God's face? How do we get to know him better? How do we come to understand him more? How do we discover his purposes?

How do we get to know anybody? Well, by spending time with them, talking to them, listening to them. That is also how we get to know God and seek his face.

We have several instances in the Bible where King David 'sought the face of the Lord'. For example, in 2 Samuel 21:1 we read: 'During the reign of David, there was a famine for three successive years; so David sought the face of the Lord.' And in Psalm 24 David tells us who has the right to come into God's presence in this way and enjoy his favour:

> *Who may ascend the hill of the Lord?*
> *Who may stand in his holy place?*
> *He who has clean hands and a pure heart,*
> *who does not lift up his soul to an idol*
> *or swear by what is false.*
> *He will receive blessing from the Lord*
> *and vindication from God his Saviour.*
> *Such is the generation of those who seek him,*
> *who seek your face, O God of Jacob.*
>
> PSALM 24:3–6

As you open up the Bible, God's word, you open a door for knowing who God is and who he wants to be for you. And as you seek God's face it is true that God will speak to you through his word! Bible reading and prayer go hand in hand. Together, they enable us to dialogue with God. You can use the words of Scripture to form your own prayers.

If you want to know what God is saying to you, to discover his will and understand his ways (as far as our finite minds are capable of grasping the thoughts of an infinite God), you will make a point of reading and trying to understand the Bible.

'Your word is a lamp to my feet and a light to my path,' exclaims the psalmist (Psalm 119:105). Let us then walk in that light!

SEEKING AND FINDING

If I can encourage more people to pray, and people to pray more, then I will have accomplished my goal in writing for you. I am convinced that our relationship with God is the most precious thing we have. Seeking his face in prayer is a privilege we want to benefit from.

I hope that you will come to realize afresh the tremendous opportunity you have to be able to approach God in prayer. The omnipotent one, the all-powerful creator God, is also your heavenly Father—he loves you and wants an intimate relationship with you.

It is a generally accepted fact that it is much easier to talk about prayer, read about prayer, and write about prayer than it is to actually pray. I hope—and pray—that the contents of this book will produce a deep desire in your heart to spend more time with God in prayer, and that you will translate that desire into action.

1

A Shopping List?

Recently I spoke to a group of young adults about prayer. In order to break the ice, I encouraged some brainstorming. Everyone was invited to answer the question, 'What is prayer?'

So that no one would feel too timid to participate, I specified that there were unlikely to be any wrong answers. We wanted to explore together the multiple facets of prayer. For it is not presenting God with a 'shopping list' of our wants. Prayer is more than just asking. Prayer is consciously spending time in God's presence, communing with him, listening to him.

DELIGHTING IN GOD

'Delight yourself in the Lord and he will give you the desires of your heart,' says Psalm 37:4. It is very easy, when reading this sentence, to forget the first clause, 'Delight yourself in the Lord', and focus on the second, 'he will give you the desires of your heart', which then comes to mean: God will give me every-thing I want! And what do I want? Wealth? Prestige? Health?

I once preached on this text at a wedding, at the request of the bride. She had asked God to give her the desire of her heart, a husband. God had graciously answered her prayer. But don't forget we are to 'delight' ourselves in him first! That is what we need to concentrate on—spending time with him, seeking his face, rejoicing in him, wanting to please him, putting him first in our lives.

God is to be our main preoccupation. 'Fix your thoughts on Jesus,' says the writer of the letter to the Hebrews (3:1). Then we will come to want what he wants. Our heart's desires will correspond to what God desires for us.

And, surely as we come to know him better and see him as he is—as the one who loved us enough to die for us; the one who has given us abundant life, eternal life; the one who wants the very best for us—then our delight in him will increase.

I believe that, whether we realize it or not, God himself is the object of our deepest desire. Nothing else will truly satisfy. And this God, who loves us, will not give us any other of our heart's desires if they are harmful to us, or if they fall short in any way of his purposes for us. And his highest purpose is to make us like Jesus.

Those whom God had already chosen,
he also set apart to become like his Son.
ROMANS 8:29 (GNB)

13

A MULTI-FACETED RELATIONSHIP OF TRUST

Prayer can be described as a dialogue with God, the creature coming before his Creator, the child coming before his heavenly Father and opening himself up, sharing intimately, confiding and listening. It has sometimes been described as 'breathing'.

One valued book on my bookshelf is *Prayer: the Christian's Vital Breath*.[3] It implies that prayer is a relationship of dependence and trust. It is through prayer that we come into God's presence and relate to him. Prayer is entering into God's purposes for us, for his Church, and for the world at large.

More than that, prayer is also a means for us to pour out our hearts to our heavenly Father. We can tell him of our joys. We can praise him for who he is. We can thank him for what he has done. We can bring our needs before him. We can invite him into our sorrows and pain.

Indeed, prayer is sometimes no more than a cry of anguish, a shout for help. 'Have mercy on me, O God,' cries David in Psalm 51:1.

Prayer is also confession. 'If we confess our sins, he is faithful and just and will forgive us our sins and purify us from all unrighteousness' (1 John 1:9). It is a means of receiving his forgiveness and cleansing.

Prayer is interceding on behalf of others. We pray for our fellow Christians, our brothers and sisters in Christ, those who are close at hand and others who may live in lands far away from us. We also pray for the salvation of those who do not yet know the Lord. Jesus tells us to pray for our enemies as well. 'Pray for those who persecute you,' he says (Matthew 5:44), 'for those who ill-treat you' (Luke 6:28).

Prayer is not hindered by distance. God is never far away. 'You are near, O Lord,' exclaims the psalmist in Psalm 119:151.

Prayer encompasses the whole of life.

But do you pray? Or do you find that you are only praying sporadically or half-heartedly? Do you want to grow in this vital aspect of your Christian life? Do you want to enter more fully into God's purposes? Do you desire a closer relationship with him?

If you are longing to deepen your relationship with God, let's begin to engage in some self-examination and re-evaluation of priorities.

2

Dependence and Devotion

What are your priorities in life? Family? Job? Church? Friends? Leisure? Whatever our priorities, they can be pretty time-consuming. Our days are so busy! Too busy? Yes, too busy, if there is no time for prayer.

If you are familiar with Martin Luther's biography, you will know that the more tasks he had to accomplish in any given day, the more time he spent in prayer. You may have come across a book by Bill Hybels with the evocative title, *Too Busy Not To Pray*.[4]

Sure, all of the other things are important, but all our priorities need to be bathed in prayer. We need to bring all of our relationships, our responsibilities and activities to God in prayer.

WHY PRAY?

Why should we pray anyway? Because the word of God tells us to: 'Be faithful in prayer' (Romans 12:12); 'Devote yourselves to prayer' (Colossians 4:2). In the context of the spiritual armour that he writes to the Ephesians about, the apostle Paul says, 'Pray in the Spirit on all occasions with all kinds of prayers and requests' (Ephesians 6:18).

True, God who is all-powerful and all-knowing doesn't need our prayers in order to act. But he wants to associate us with his work. He wants us to pray.

Carmen, a member of our church, is a missionary in Mozambique. She works among people who have leprosy. Imagine Carmen trying to do God's work without the prayer support of her church!

If the apostle Paul asked for prayer—for example in his letter to the Colossians, where he writes, 'Pray for us, too, that God may open a door for our message, so that we may proclaim the mystery of Christ... Pray that I may proclaim it clearly...' (Colossians 4:3, 4) —then surely God's servants still need prayer today.

We pray because we are dependent on God. Jesus says, 'Apart from me you can do nothing' (John 15:5). Prayer is a way of recognizing and acknowledging our dependence.

'You do not have, because you do not ask God,' writes James in his letter (James 4:2b). That's pretty down to earth, isn't it? And it's quite logical. It's really the corollary to what Jesus said: 'Ask and it will be given to you; seek and you will find; knock and the door will be opened to you' (Matthew 7:7; Luke 11:9).

It is no good just wishing or hoping for something if we haven't asked God for it. He wants us to ask. Our heavenly Father longs to pour out his blessings on his children. If only we would ask!

'You may ask me for anything in my name and I will do it,' says Jesus (John 14:14). The apostle John writes, 'This is the confidence we have in approaching God: that if we ask anything according to his will, he hears us. And if we know that he hears us—whatever we ask—we know that we have what we asked of him' (1 John 5:14–15).

GLORIFYING GOD

It is interesting to see what reason Jesus gives for answering our prayers. He says in John 14:13, 'I will do whatever you ask in my name, *so that the Son may bring glory to the Father*' (emphasis added), or 'that the Father may be glorified' (KJV).

Surely that is an excellent reason for praying—that God may be glorified! I wonder how often this is in our minds when we pray. Or are we so caught up with our own needs and desires that we cannot see beyond them?

Consciously try to bring Jesus into all that you do. He cares about every part of your life—your feelings and desires, your health, your relationships, your responsibilities, your activities, your professional life, your family life, your times of recreation, your hobbies.

Talk to him about all that makes up your life. Open yourself up to him. Ask for his guidance in planning and choosing. Share your thoughts with him. Seek his face. Renew yourself in him. You will be amazed at the changes for good in your life in Christ.

How did Jesus renew himself spiritually? By spending time alone with his Father. We read: 'He went up on a mountainside by himself to pray. When evening came, he was there alone' (Matthew 14:23). 'Jesus often withdrew to lonely places and prayed' (Luke 5:16). 'Jesus went out to a mountainside to pray, and spent the night praying to God' (Luke 6:12).

How much quiet do you have in your day? We live in a noisy world of traffic, TV, radio, phone, all kinds of electronic devices. Do you ever switch them off in order to be quiet with God?

Disquiet and unrest can also be the result of a cluttered mind. Discipline is a word we do not tend to like very much, but the days run more smoothly and are more conducive to prayer if we try to order our lives a bit. I remember once remarking to one of our teenage boys that the state of his bedroom reflected the muddle inside of him. He agreed!

Do you have a special place—a 'lonely place'—where you meet with God? 'When you pray,' says Jesus, 'go into your room, close the door and pray to your Father who is unseen. Then your Father, who sees what is done in secret, will reward you' (Matthew 6:6).

Like you, I am busy. It is not always easy to find the space to be alone with God. I remember participating in a youth camp once, where hustle and bustle seemed to be the order of the day (and night!). I would climb on to a top bunk in the dormitory and, turning my back to the noise and my face to the wall, would commune with God, although briefly.

I have learned that I need, each day, to make time and place for prayer. How can we truly live without seeking a close relationship with God—to meet with him, to listen and to share with him? It is a well-known fact that Susannah Wesley, in a busy household and with many children, would pull her apron over her head in order to find the privacy to pray. When she did this, she knew she would not be disturbed or interrupted.

Since our two children grew up and moved away from home, I now have the luxury of a study to work in. This is usually where I meet with God at the start of each new day and where I often return to lift my heart to him during the day's different occupations.

I have found other prayer places nearby. The place where I live in France has been for generations a market gardening town. Often, in the summer, I rise early to seek God's face and commune with him during an early morning walk. To see the risen sun slanting across rows of fresh green lettuces standing out against the rich brown earth gives me much pleasure and causes me to thank the Lord.

Sometimes I stroll along the bank of a river running through our village. As swallows sweep and dive over the rapids, and butterflies flit daintily around the buddleia, I sit on a rock overhanging the water and talk to God. At other times I read his word and pray in some shady nook in our garden.

Wherever you live, whether in a small village, or in the country, or in a bustling city—do not be content just to read this book on prayer. Make time in your busy days; find your own quiet place—and pray!

3

'Teach Us to Pray'

I chose the title of this chapter advisedly—'Teach Us to Pray'—for I want us to come before the Lord together to learn of him. I am not setting myself up as one who is an authority on the subject, or as one who knows all about it. I don't claim to have got to the bottom of the mystery or to have all the answers to the very real problems we sometimes encounter when we pray. We are learning together.

Sometimes I feel I understand less now, with nearly fifty years of Christian life behind me, than I did when I was a child. It was simple then. And, in one way, it is simple now. 'Ask and it shall be given to you,' says Jesus (Matthew 7:7). What could be simpler than that?

'Teach us to pray' is, you will remember, the request the disciples brought to Jesus. Nowhere in the Gospels do we read that they asked Jesus to teach them to preach, to evangelize, to heal the sick, to cast out demons. They have already been out doing all of that.

No, they wanted to learn to pray. And what sparked their request? His example.

We read in the Gospel accounts that before the disciples asked Jesus to teach them to pray, they had already on several occasions watched him pray.

'Once when Jesus was praying in private and his disciples were with him…' (Luke 9:18). 'He took Peter, John and James with him and went up on to a mountain to pray' (Luke 9:28).

They had observed his prayer life, how during his busy schedule he would get up early, while it was still dark, and spend long hours alone with his Father in prayer. 'We want to pray like that,' they thought. 'We want this same unbroken communion with the Father.'

And at the beginning of Luke 11, we read: 'One day Jesus was praying in a certain place. When he finished, one of his disciples said to him, "Lord, teach us to pray…"'

A RELATIONSHIP, NOT A TECHNIQUE

G. Campbell Morgan, in a small volume entitled *The Practice of Prayer*, points out that the disciples did not ask Jesus to teach them *how* to pray. 'Teach us *to* pray' was their request.[5]

As I began to think about this, I realized what an important distinction there is between these two concepts, particularly in our day and age, which sports an abundance of 'Know how…' and 'How to…' books, 'Twelve step' programs, and others.

'Prayer changes things…' is a little chorus we used to sing when I was a child. Whenever I sang it, I had a nagging doubt about the accuracy of the words: it is not my prayer that changes anything; it is the one to whom I pray, the almighty, omnipotent God. He hears; he answers; he acts. He is to be our focus.

The disciples did not ask Jesus to provide them with some kind of technique for formulating prayers or for getting snappy answers. Neither did they want him to show them which posture might be appropriate for addressing the Almighty.

They were not caught up with secondary issues. They were concerned with the essentials. They meant business. They wanted to pray—really pray!

They were asking Jesus, whom they had so often observed in deep communion with his Father, to help them approach the one who was also their heavenly Father, and develop their relationship with him, a relationship of love.

Our Father in heaven,
hallowed be your name,
your kingdom come, your will be done
on earth as it is in heaven.
Give us today our daily bread.
Forgive us our debts,
as we also have forgiven our debtors.
And lead us not into temptation,
but deliver us from the evil one.

MATTHEW 6:9–13

In this model prayer that Jesus gave to the disciples, God remains the focus. The disciples were—as are we—to pray to the Father in heaven.

We ask first of all that his 'holy name be honoured' (GNB), revered, respected. We are to give God his rightful place.

Even though this prayer puts God's interests first, surely it is also to our advantage, if we are in tune with him, that his 'kingdom come'.

Next, Jesus told his followers to ask that their own needs be met, the basic necessities of life first of all: 'Give us each day our daily bread.'

Then we are instructed to pray for our moral and spiritual needs—for forgiveness from sin, and for deliverance from temptation.

'Teach us to pray.' Therein lie lessons for a lifetime. We shall never have finished learning all that the Lord has to teach us about prayer.

We go on to greater and even more glorious dis-coveries if we continue learning about prayer. I do not know where you are in this school of prayer, this great adventure, but I want to encourage you to persevere, to continue, and above all, to pray!

4

A Spark

Whatever you ask for in prayer, believe that you have received it and it will be yours.

MARK 11:24

THE SAME THE WORLD OVER

Margie and Alfred are a married couple who were separated when we first knew them. A hopeless situation? It appeared so. Yet, people prayed for them. God intervened. Margie and Alfred have now been back together for some time, working through their problems together and enjoying a harmonious marriage.

Yasukazu, from a Buddhist background in Japan, started coming to our church with his Christian wife a few years ago. We began to pray for his conversion. One Sunday, during the service, Yasukazu understood that God loved him enough to die for him and he accepted Jesus as his Saviour. He testified to his faith through baptism six months later.

Nana, a Ghanaian member of our church, phoned me, rejoicing and praising the Lord because she had successfully defended her thesis and was now 'by the grace of God, a qualified social worker'. Her thesis was exceptionally well received by the examiners, who praised her for her excellent work. Nana, who knew that the church had been praying, felt supported and upheld throughout the ordeal, and was eager to thank us for our prayers.

GOD ANSWERS PRAYER!

In writing about prayer, I am aiming to seek and to express something *fresh* that will really motivate people to pray. A line of a chorus says, 'It only takes a spark to get a fire going.'[6] What is the 'spark' that gets people praying?

True, we have a great deal of teaching about prayer in the Bible. We see many examples of prayer in the Old Testament. We see Jesus and his life of prayer in the Gospels. We have some wonderful recorded prayers of the apostle Paul in the epistles… and so it goes on.

But what is the spark that is going to set us off? Sometimes we need something to which we can relate personally. And what is more encouraging to us, what inspires us to pray more than to see answers to prayer, like those answers given to Margie and Alfred and others I have mentioned?

I remember how one morning, after speaking some unkind, thoughtless words to someone, I was feeling very remorseful. I turned to the Lord to confess and repent; and I asked him to work for good in that particular relationship. The healing and reconciliation he brought that same day were overwhelming. Truly he 'is able to do immeasurably more than all we ask or imagine' (Ephesians 3:20).

When we experience answers to prayer in our own lives, or when we see God working in the lives of other people, we are encouraged to persevere to seek his face in prayer. And that is just what God wants us to do.

In Luke 18:1–8, Jesus told his disciples a parable to show them that they should always pray and not give up: an unjust judge, who did not fear God and who did not care about people, was pestered so much by a widow that, in order to get rid of her, he eventually intervened on her behalf, so that justice might be done for her. The point of the parable is this: if even an unjust, unloving judge eventually yields to a person's repeated implorations, how much more will a loving God delight to answer the prayers of his children. We are encouraged to persist in prayer even when we might be tempted to give up.

A DIFFICULTY

Sometimes we begin to feel that we've prayed long and hard, but God doesn't seem to hear our prayers. At any rate, he does not seem to be answering. This is where we run into difficulty and temptation to doubt.

There may be things we pray for which we can be absolutely sure are according to God's will. We have already said that we can pray that God might be glorified. 'I will glorify your name forever,' exclaims David in Psalm 86. Jesus himself prays, 'Father... glorify your Son, that your Son may glorify you' (John 17:1).

So let us pray in faith that God will be glorified, for we know that prayer will be answered.

We know too that God does not want 'anyone to perish, but everyone to come to repentance' (2 Peter 3:9). So let us pray, believing, for people to turn to God in repentance and faith.

If you are sure you are praying in accordance with God's will, persevere in prayer. Continue in prayer; he will answer. Do not give up; do not despair.

GOD'S WAYS ARE BEST

However, there may be things we pray for, and we are not sure that it is God's will to grant us those things, those longings, those desires. I do not think it is a cop-out to say, as Jesus did, 'Lord, this is what I'm asking for. Nevertheless, not my will, but yours be done.'

God has given people freedom of choice. He will not force them to do his will, and he is often grieved by their rebelliousness. We have an example in the book of Jeremiah, where through the mouth of his prophet, God addresses his people: 'Turn from your evil ways... and reform your ways and your actions' (Jeremiah 18:11b). In the following verse, the people reply, 'We will continue with our own plans; each of us will follow the stubbornness of his evil heart.'

God's sovereignty and our responsibility are like two parallel lines running throughout the Bible. We, finite creatures that we are, cannot always reconcile these two truths.

But we know that God is perfectly just, and we can trust him. Also, we do not know the whole story. God alone can see the end from the beginning.

God's ways are far above our ways. His ways are best. 'My thoughts are not your thoughts, neither are your ways my ways, declares the Lord. As the heavens are higher than the earth, so are my ways higher than your ways and my thoughts than your thoughts' (Isaiah 55:8–9).

How can we, sinful, finite creatures that we are, pretend to understand the mind of God? However, we can always come to him and share with him what is on our heart. Sometimes we need just to submit to him and leave everything in his hands, trusting that he will work things out, knowing that he loves us and wants the best for us.

INNER PEACE

Even if God's ways do not correspond to what you would necessarily personally desire, knowing that his ways are best takes the edge off any pain involved in submitting to his will, and gives a deep-down peace. Peace amid the pain, joy in trials—strange paradox of the Christian faith, and yet a reality when we live for God and eternal values, rather than for this life alone.

But this peace and joy may not come without a struggle, because even though God's ways are best, they are often not the easiest and not what we would naturally have chosen. We need to have our eyes opened to God's ultimate purposes and remember that, through the circumstances of our lives, he is making and moulding us into the image of Christ.

Sometimes we find it difficult to look beyond instant gratification and immediate pleasure. Can't we trust God to do what is best?

LIKE A WEANED CHILD

Maybe our struggling is what the psalmist had in mind when, in Psalm 131:2, he talks about weaning: 'I have stilled and quieted my soul; like a weaned child with its mother, like a weaned child is my soul within me.'

Commenting on this psalm, Sinclair Ferguson describes the struggles and trauma of the weaning process and says:

True contentment is not the same thing as getting whatever we want; it is submitting to the Lord's will and learning to desire what he does… When we are weaned as infants, we lose the milk we desire in order to receive the solid food we need… So too in the world of the spirit, the weaning that brings us to contentment in the Lord takes place through loss. Every experience in life with which we are deprived of what we naturally want becomes the means by which our Father gives us what he knows we really need.[7]

If it is God's purpose to make us like Jesus, then our aim in life should be to glorify our heavenly Father through trusting him, obeying him and joyfully submitting to his perfect will.

'Your will be done.' Just four words, but four words that can transform our whole attitude to prayer. Words, however, which are not all that easy to say—and mean.

We can be so intent on getting our own way that yielding our will to that of another seems quite out of the question—unless of course we believe that the 'Other' loves us with a steadfast, everlasting love and wants the very best for us! Then we might be glad to leave him to work things out according to his perfect will.

Do we know him? Do we love him? If yes, then can we not trust him to know best? Of course, the 'best' may not be the easiest or the most pleasant. When Jesus uttered these words, 'Your will be done', they led him to the cross.

God may take us through an experience of dying—to ourselves, to our own selfish desires—in order to raise us up to a life of fulfilment and satisfaction in him.

There is not in the world a kind of life more sweet and delightful than that of a continual conversation with God.
BROTHER LAWRENCE

5

All the Time

The apostle Paul wrote, 'Pray continually' (1 Thessalonians 5:1), or as some other translations have it, 'Pray all the time' (THE MESSAGE); 'Pray without ceasing' (KJV); 'Always keep on praying' (LB). Well, how do we do that? Surely it's a bit unrealistic! How can you 'pray without ceasing', 'continually', 'all the time', when you have a busy schedule, young children to look after, or other work that takes all your thought and concentration?

If we have already come to realize that prayer is relating with God and seeking his face, then this intimacy we have with him will mean that we are in his presence at all times, whatever else we are engaged in. God has promised that he will never leave us or forsake us. He is always with us. We are with him.

As you go about your daily routine, there will be times that you may wish to consult him about some decision you have to make, to ask his guidance. There may be times that you will cry out to him in pain, seeking his comfort or his strength. At other times, you will just lift your heart to him in praise and adoration.

As Leon Morris says in his commentary on Thessalonians:

It is not possible for us to spend all our time with the words of prayer on our lips, but it is possible for us to be all our days in the spirit of prayer, realizing our dependence on God for all that we have and are, realizing something of his presence with us wherever we may be, and yielding ourselves continually to him for the doing of his will.[8]

This leads us to consider two aspects of prayer that we have not really talked about yet, except perhaps implicitly in passing. The first of these is those prayers that are commonly known as 'telegraphic' or 'arrow' prayers. The second is 'continual praying', which relates to a book entitled *The Practice of the Presence of God*.

ARROW PRAYERS

A good example of an 'arrow' prayer is found early in the book of Nehemiah. We find Nehemiah, who had identified himself at the end of the previous chapter as 'cupbearer to the king', in the presence of King Artaxerxes.

'I took the wine and gave it to the king,' he relates (Nehemiah 2:1).

The king notices the expression on Nehemiah's face, and asks him why he is so sad. Rather fearfully, Nehemiah explains that his sadness is due to the fact that Jerusalem had been destroyed.

The king then asks, 'What is it you want?' (2:4). Here we see Nehemiah, already engaged in conversation with the king, offer up a prayer to the Lord before replying. 'I prayed to the God of heaven,' he says, 'and I answered the king.'

His prayer was completely unknown by King Artaxerxes, but it resulted in Nehemiah's request being granted.

Isn't it wonderful to have such a resource as prayer? Whatever situation you find yourself in, you can always seek God's direction.

As you listen to the news or read the newspaper, you can intercede on behalf of those who are oppressed and abused, and pray for the rulers of nations, or for countries where there is conflict or disaster. The apostle Paul urges us to pray 'for kings and all those in authority' (1 Timothy 2:1–2).

You can count on God's strength in your weakness, his comfort in your suffering, his wisdom in your decision-making and in your responsibilities. Do not neglect this upward glance as you go about your daily business.

PRACTISING THE PRESENCE OF GOD—
A CONTINUAL CONVERSATION

The other aspect of prayer we want to consider is that continuous praying which is the subject of a wonderful little book by a 17th-century French monk by the name of Brother Lawrence, entitled *The Practice of the Presence of God*.

I first discovered Brother Lawrence's book many

years ago in a cathedral bookshop in England. My copy is now well worn and underlined in many places. It consists mainly of conversations Brother Lawrence had and letters he wrote between 1666, when he first entered a Carmelite community in Paris, and 1691, the date of his death.

He made himself aware of God's presence 'by continually conversing with him', and Brother Lawrence encourages his readers to 'live in a continual sense of his presence'.

He suggests that we ought to 'seek our satisfaction only in the fulfilling of [God's] will, whether he lead us by suffering or by consolation, for all would be equal to a soul truly resigned'.

Am I 'a soul truly resigned'? I wonder. Are you?

Counting on God's grace and forgiveness, Brother Lawrence's actions sprang out of his love for God. He 'was pleased when he could take up a straw from the ground for the love of God, seeking him only and nothing else, not even his gifts'.

Brother Lawrence exhorts us 'once for all, heartily to put our whole trust in God, and make a total surrender of ourselves to him', and encourages us to 'act with God in the greatest simplicity, speaking to him frankly and plainly, and imploring his assistance in our affairs just as they happen'.

Brother Lawrence wrote that he did not naturally like his appointed work in the monastery kitchen at all; however, that work was completely transformed for him because he did it out of his love for God and a consciousness of God's presence with him.

He describes his awareness of God's presence as 'an habitual, silent, and secret conversation of the soul with God'. He exclaims: 'There is not in the world a kind of life more sweet and delightful than that of a continual conversation with God.'

And we shall leave Brother Lawrence to give us this final exhortation: 'Lift up your heart to him.'[9]

6

Standing Firm

In the morning, O Lord, you hear my voice; in the morning I lay my request before you and wait in expectation.

PSALM 5:1–3

We must 'pray without ceasing', and we also need discipline in our prayer life. We need to set aside special times to seek God's face in prayer.

How many times have you been asked to pray for someone or something which has afterwards immediately slipped your mind? And worse, how many times have you casually said, 'I'll pray for you', or 'I'll pray about that', and then thought no more about it? To remedy this rather irresponsible attitude to intercession, we need to discipline ourselves and set aside specific times for prayer.

I remember an incident many years ago when I was a student in Liverpool. Jill, a Christian friend, was sharing with me some of her problems related to the fact that she was diabetic. A few days later, she was rejoicing that she felt much better, and she asked me point blank, 'Did you pray for me?'

I was very ashamed to realize and to have to admit

that I had not remembered her difficulties, nor prayed about them. That interaction taught me a lesson. Now, when anyone shares a problem with me, I make a point of taking it to the Lord in prayer.

It could be useful to have a prayer list or a journal in which to jot down the names of people or the matters you commit to pray for. Or you might write a person's name or an event against a date on the calendar or in your diary, in order to remind you to pray on that particular day. There may be a Bible verse that would correspond to a request you wish to make on someone's behalf. In that case, you could write the person's name in the margin of your Bible next to that verse. I'm sure you can think of practical ways in which to give your memory a little jog.

In his letter to the Colossians, the apostle Paul gives us a wonderful example of an intercessor in the person of Epaphras who, he says, 'is always wrestling in prayer for you, that you may stand firm in all the will of God, mature and fully assured' (Colossians 4:12).

How encouraging for the Christians in Colossae to know that they were being prayed for in that way! Wouldn't you like to know that someone was praying for you like that? And there is nothing to stop you 'wrestling in prayer' in such a way, so that others may stand firm in the faith.

IN THE MORNING

Give ear to my words, O Lord,
consider my sighing.
Listen to my cry for help,
my king and my God,
for to you I pray.
In the morning, O Lord, you hear my voice;
in the morning I lay my requests before you
and wait in expectation.

PSALM 5:1–3

How good it is to start the morning with God, as did David, the author of this psalm; to come consciously into his presence and commit the new day to him! I realize that spending time in prayer first thing in the morning may not be practical or even possible for everyone. It is up to each of us to determine the best time and place for us to have this special meeting with God.

However, surely, whatever our schedule or responsibilities might be, we can lift our hearts and thoughts to him at the beginning of each day, deliberately handing the new day over to him.

It does not even need to be articulate, well-expressed prayer. In Psalm 5, quoted above, David seems to communicate initially by sighs: 'Consider my sighing,' he says in the first verse. God could see into his heart and knew his inmost thoughts and his needs.

We have a wonderful promise and assurance in the New Testament, too, in Paul's letter to the Romans, where we read: 'We do not know what we ought to pray for, but the Spirit himself intercedes for us with groans that words cannot express. And he who searches our hearts knows the mind of the Spirit, because the Spirit intercedes for the saints in accordance with God's will' (Romans 8:26–27).

In Psalm 5:2, David prays: 'Listen to my cry for help, my king and my God.' He addresses the Lord as 'my king and my God', implying an intimate relationship with God, while at the same time recognizing and acknowledging God's authority.

You too can come before the great creator God, king of the universe, and make your requests to him, because this sovereign Lord is also your heavenly Father and your Saviour.

PRAYING WITH EXPECTATION

In Psalm 5 there is a sense of expectancy about David's prayer: 'I lay my requests before you and wait in expectation' (v. 3).

He prays and then waits to see what God will do. Do you have this same sense of expectation and anticipation?

Having established that we need to find a time for our special meeting with God, whether this is first thing in the morning or at some other, more convenient time of the day or night, let us be faithful in keeping our appointment with him. And let us pray with expectation, trusting God to answer us!

7

Boldness

HOW CAN GOD UNDERSTAND ME?

Have you ever been tempted to wonder, as you were praying, whether such a great, almighty, sovereign, holy God could possibly understand you, insignificant, earthbound creature that you are? I well remember doubts like these forming in my mind one day.

I was walking along a street in Geneva, in the direction of the lake. As I walked, I prayed. And as I prayed, I began dialoguing with myself.

'It just cannot be possible,' I said to myself, 'that God, who is so completely "other", and who is far off, in heaven, should come down to my level. How can he possibly understand me? How can he relate to my needs? How can he hear my prayers?'

At that point, the full force of the amazing truth of the Incarnation struck me so hard that it brought me to a halt. This transcendent God understands me perfectly, not only because he created me ('You created my inmost being; you knit me together in my mother's womb,' exclaims David, in Psalm 139) but also because he became *like* me. God who is far off—in heaven—came near, coming down to earth in the person of Jesus Christ. God, who is completely 'other', became one of us. He 'became flesh and lived among us' (John 1:14, NRSV).

Wow! I could show you the exact spot on that street in Geneva where this realization hit me. It was just as I was about to cross the road outside the Natural History Museum. I remember it so distinctly because that is where I was overwhelmed by such a revelation that I remained as if rooted to the ground.

God identified fully with us through becoming man. He had a body, like ours. He took upon himself the weakest, most fragile, most vulnerable human form, that of a newborn baby. And where was this baby born? In a stable!

How could God humble himself to such an extent? Throughout his life on this earth, he identified fully with us, sinful human beings, to the point of dying in our place. The apostle Paul expresses it graphically in his letter to the Philippians. He tells them that their attitude should be the same as that of Christ Jesus:

> *Who, being in very nature God,*
> *did not consider equality with God*
> *something to be grasped,*
> *but made himself nothing,*
> *taking the very nature of a servant,*
> *being made in human likeness,*
> *And being found in appearance as a man,*
> *he humbled himself and became obedient to death—*
> *even death on a cross!*
>
> PHILIPPIANS 2:5–8

We only have to read the Gospel accounts to see something of Christ's life on earth and to understand the extent to which he identified with sinful humanity: his birth in Bethlehem, where his mother 'wrapped him in cloths and placed him in a manger because there was no room for them in the inn' (Luke 2:7). How could the omnipotent God humble himself to such a degree?

And then, before beginning his ministry, his baptism, a significant act, is recorded for us in Matthew 3:13–17. Significant, because this was a baptism of repentance. But Jesus, who was sinless, had no need to repent. It was for that very reason that John the Baptist protested, not wanting to baptize him. So why then was Jesus baptized? In order to identify fully with the sinful people he had come to save.

We see too in the Gospels that, like us, he had a human family. His 'mother and brothers' are mentioned in Mark 3:31–32. As he was teaching in the synagogue in Nazareth, the people were astonished at his wisdom and exclaimed, 'Isn't this the carpenter's son? Isn't his mother's name Mary, and aren't his brothers James, Joseph, Simon and Judas? Aren't all his sisters with us?' (Matthew 13:55–56).

Like us, he was hungry: 'After fasting for forty days and forty nights, he was hungry' (Matthew 4:2).

Like us, he was thirsty: 'Jesus said, "I am thirsty"' (John 19:28).

We know too that Jesus wept when he came before the tomb of Lazarus (John 11:35).

And, like us, he needed sleep. Remember the storm on Lake Galilee, when the disciples were so afraid? What was Jesus doing just then? We read in Matthew 8:24: 'Jesus was sleeping.'

Another very human need he had was that of friends. Do you remember why Jesus chose his disciples? Yes, true, he chose them so they might teach and preach and cast out demons and heal the sick. But first and foremost, why did he choose them? We read in Mark 3:14: 'He appointed twelve—designating them apostles—*that they might be with him*' (emphasis added).

We have a wonderful example of that in the person of Mary, who 'sat at the Lord's feet and listened to what he said': Jesus said she had 'chosen what is better' (Luke 10:38–42). He sought human companionship, just as we do.

And like us, but to a far greater degree, he faced human injustice. 'He was despised and rejected by men... He was oppressed and afflicted' (Isaiah 53:3, 7).

Jesus identified with us in all aspects of our humanity. For that reason, he is able to understand us. For that reason, he knows from experience 'how we are formed, he remembers that we are dust' (Psalm 103:14).

HIGH PRIEST AND SON OF GOD

In the letter to the Hebrews, we read this about Jesus:

He had to be made like his brothers in every way, in order that he might become a faithful and merciful high priest in service to God, and that he might make atonement for the sins of the people.

Because he himself suffered when he was tempted, Jesus is able to help those who are being tempted... Therefore, since we have a great high priest who has gone through the heavens, Jesus the Son of God, let us hold firmly to the faith we profess.

For we do not have a high priest who is unable to sympathize with our weaknesses, but we have One who has been tempted in every way, just as we are—yet was without sin.

Let us then approach the throne of grace with confidence, so that we may receive mercy and find grace to help us in our time of need.

HEBREWS 2:17–18; 4:14–16

Jesus is called both 'high priest' and 'Son of God'. This means that Jesus represents human beings before God on the one hand, and God before human beings on the other. In order to be the perfect high priest, Jesus had to become human and identify fully with us. These verses show that Jesus understands our weaknesses, that he bears our sin, and that he sympathizes with us and intercedes for us.

Now, however, we are up against a great theological question regarding ourselves: how can a sinful human being come into the presence of a holy God, whose 'eyes are too pure to look on evil' (Habakkuk 1:13)?

The psalmist asks this very question in Psalm 24:3: 'Who may ascend the hill of the Lord? Who may stand in his holy place?'

The psalmist answers his own question later in the same psalm: 'He who has clean hands and a pure heart' (24:4) may approach God. But none of us has 'clean hands and a pure heart'.

At this point we see that Jesus went all the way in his identification with us. 'The wages of sin is death,' writes the apostle Paul (Romans 6:23). We deserved to die, because of our sin. But Jesus died in our place. He willingly received the punishment that we deserved. He took upon himself our sin, and bore the punishment for it, so that we might be clothed, as it were, in his righteousness.

'God made him who had no sin to be sin for us, so that in him we might become the righteousness of God' (2 Corinthians 5:21). Clothed in the righteousness of Christ, with 'clean hands and a pure heart', we can freely, boldly and confidently enter the presence of God.

Remember my thoughts described earlier, as I walked toward Lake Geneva. 'It just cannot be possible,' I said to myself, 'that God, who is so completely "other", and who is far off, in heaven, should come down to my level. How can he possibly understand me? How can he relate to my needs? How can he hear my prayers?'

If you have doubts like mine, you need not hold on to them! God is not too distant to understand your prayers. Do not ever think that God cannot identify with your needs, your desires, your problems.

Remember instead that he went all out in his identification with you, and that he has been tempted in every way you are. Therefore, you can approach the throne of grace with boldness, confident that God understands you perfectly, that he loves you and that he will act on your behalf.

8

Take It to the Lord

He who did not spare his own Son, but gave him up
for us all—how will he not also, along with him,
graciously give us all things?

ROMANS 8:32

I was visiting my mother in hospital near Bristol. She
was dying. Overcome by emotion, I left her room
momentarily to recover myself.

In the corridor, a woman kindly asked me what was
wrong. On sharing with her the cause of my distress,
she 'comforted' me in the only way she knew how:
'Go and have a nice cup of tea,' was her very British
suggestion!

Now this woman was a stranger to me. Her lack of
sensitivity amused me more than anything. But have
you ever had the experience—the painful experience
—of sharing a problem or deep concern with a dear
and trusted friend, only to find that your friend fell far
short of responding in the way that you had hoped?
The disappointment and sense of rejection were
probably pretty devastating. And your initial reaction
would hardly be one of thanksgiving!

And yet, maybe in the long run you will end up giving thanks. For you may come to realize, as I did, that human comfort—even at its best—cannot compare with the consolation Jesus Christ can offer. Human understanding—even at its deepest—cannot equal the knowledge God has of you, for as we saw in the previous chapter, he made you, he became like you, and not only does he know all about you, but he knows you intimately, through and through.

David exclaims in Psalm 139:1–4, 13, 15:

O Lord, you have searched me and you know me. You know when I sit and when I rise; you perceive my thoughts from afar. You discern my going out and my lying down; you are familiar with all my ways. Before a word is on my tongue you know it completely, O Lord…

For you created my inmost being; you knit me together in my mother's womb… My frame was not hidden from you when I was made in the secret place. When I was woven together in the depths of the earth, your eyes saw my unformed body…

GOD'S LOVE

The love and affection of a friend can in no way measure up to God's love for you, which he demonstrated at infinite cost, as we are told in Romans 5:8: 'God demonstrates his own love for us in this: While we were still sinners, Christ died for us.' And, in

John 3:16: 'God so loved the world that he gave his one and only Son, that whoever believes in him shall not perish but have eternal life.'

He loves you 'with an everlasting love' (Jeremiah 31:3).

SYMPATHY, TENDERNESS AND AFFECTION

Likewise, if you are looking for sympathy, tenderness, affection, it is in Jesus that you will find them. In Zechariah's song, we read of 'the tender mercy of our God' (Luke 1:78).

The psalmist tells us, 'As a father has compassion on his children, so the Lord has compassion on those who fear him' (Psalm 103:13).

And the Lord says, through the words of the prophet Isaiah, 'As a mother comforts her child, so will I comfort you' (Isaiah 66:13).

You and I must count on God's love, for his love never fails. Your cause for thanksgiving then is that a painful situation has forced you to turn to the Lord— the only one who can meet your deepest needs—and experience his love, his compassion, his comfort, his tenderness, and his understanding.

He, who loved you enough to die for you, will surely give you all that you truly need. 'He who did not spare his own Son,' writes the apostle Paul to the Romans, 'but gave him up for us all—how will he not also, along with him, graciously give us all things' (Romans 8:32).

God has already given us the best, that which is dearest to his heart, that which cost him the most. So we can be absolutely sure that he will also give us everything else we need. Indeed we have a promise to that end in the New Testament: 'My God will meet all your needs according to his glorious riches in Christ Jesus' (Philippians 4:19).

GOD HEARS OUR CRY

He will hear your cry for help and respond as no human friend could ever do. Psalm 107 recounts many instances of God's deliverances. The following refrain runs throughout the psalm: 'They cried out to the Lord in their trouble, and he delivered them from their distress.'

In other psalms we read: 'I love the Lord, for he heard my voice; he heard my cry for mercy... When I was in great need, he saved me' (Psalm 116:1, 6); 'In my anguish I cried to the Lord, and he answered by setting me free' (Psalm 118:5); and Psalm 120:1: 'I call on the Lord in my distress, and he answers me.'

Working through hurts in my own life and opening myself up to God's love and gracious provision, I was struck by the following words of the psalmist: 'You, Lord, are all I have, and you give me all I need' (Psalm 16:5, GNB), and 'When I look beside me, I see that there is no one to help me, no one to protect me. No one cares for me. Lord, I cry to you for help; you, Lord, are my protector; you are all I want in this life' (Psalm 142:4–5, GNB).

The above thoughts and feelings and the assurance I came to from verses from God's word, such as the ones already quoted, inspired me to write the following lines:

Look up

When friendship fails
And no one cares
That sorrow crushes me,
Think of the nails:
There's One who shares
The pain and agony.

Why look elsewhere
To find the love
That only he can give?
In deep despair,
Just glance above—
Look up at him and live.

A warm embrace,
A loving touch—
When these things are denied,
By God's own grace
I have so much
And in his peace abide.

Why comfort seek
From one who'll fall,
A loved one though he be?

When I am weak,
I can do all
Through Christ who strengthens me.

He's all I have,
This precious Friend.
His is the voice I heed.
Whate'er I crave,
I can depend
On him to meet my need.

9

Prayer and Faith

We live by faith, not by sight.

2 CORINTHIANS 5:7

You have perhaps had the experience of praying fervently for something over a long period of time. There seem to be many obstacles to your prayers being answered, and things may look pretty hopeless. Little by little, you begin to think that God is never going to answer, and maybe you begin to doubt whether he really can.

There are situations in life that may cause you to despair. You may have been praying for the conversion of a loved one for many years, and he still seems far away from God. You may have been praying for someone with an addiction or a dependency problem and see no signs of deliverance.

We can get to the point in our praying when we no longer believe that God can or will answer. The situation is just too complex, too difficult.

TOO DIFFICULT FOR GOD?

I have been praying for a long time about one of those humanly-speaking impossible situations. My degree of faith, I must confess, has fluctuated during this time. I remember some time ago feeling utter despair, at which point my husband said to me, 'Don't reckon without God.'

Four little words—'Don't reckon without God'— but they made all the difference. Hope was reborn. And, since then, there has always been a flicker of hope along with my vacillating faith.

Just before Christmas the year my husband said those words to me, a member of my Bible study group shared with us a short meditation from Isaiah 42:3, where we find these encouraging words: 'A bruised reed he will not break and a smouldering wick he will not snuff out.'

'A bruised reed' is *almost* broken, but not quite. There is still hope. 'A smouldering wick' is *almost* extinguished, but not quite. There is still hope. There is always hope in God!

EVERYTHING IS POSSIBLE

One night I was challenged about my 'little faith.' I could only say, as did the father we read about in Mark 9:24, 'I believe; help my unbelief' (NRSV). Do you remember the incident I'm referring to, recorded in Mark 9:12–37?

Jesus comes down from the Mount of Transfiguration with Peter, James and John to find the other disciples surrounded by a crowd, the teachers of the law arguing with them.

When Jesus asks what is going on, a man in the crowd tells him that the disciples are unable to drive out a spirit that has possessed his son. 'Bring the boy to me,' says Jesus.

After explaining how the boy has been afflicted since his childhood, the father then begs, 'If you can do anything, take pity on us and help us.'

Jesus picks up on this, and repeats, 'If you can?' He then goes on to say, 'Everything is possible for him who believes.'

Then the father utters those words we have already referred to: 'I do believe; help me overcome my unbelief', whereupon Jesus drives out the spirit.

As soon as I had echoed those same words, I had the conviction that God can and will work in the matter I have been praying about, bringing deliverance and victory over sin. The following morning I read some of the Gospel accounts of Jesus' ministry, rediscovering the wonder of the miracles—and, at the same time, the disciples' little faith.

FAITH, AND LACK OF IT

In Matthew 6:30, Jesus challenges his followers by saying that, if God clothes the flowers, 'will he not much more clothe you, O you of little faith?'

In another incident, recounted for us in Matthew 14, Jesus enables Peter to walk on the water. All goes well until Peter becomes aware of the wind, and then, terrified, he begins to sink.

'Lord, save me!' he cries.

As Jesus reaches out his hand to catch him, he exclaims: 'You of little faith, why did you doubt?'

In Mark's Gospel, after calming the storm on the lake, Jesus says to his disciples: 'Why are you so afraid? Do you still have no faith?' (Mark 4:40).

One of the most sobering expressions relative to unbelief is when Jesus, back in his home town, 'did not do many miracles there because of their lack of faith' (Matthew 13:58).

COMMENDED FOR FAITH

But we do not want to stress just the negative aspect— the *lack* of faith. There are many instances in the Bible where Jesus *commends* people's faith.

Of the centurion in Matthew 8, Jesus says, 'I have not found anyone in Israel with such great faith' (Matthew 8:10).

To the 'woman who had been subject to bleeding for twelve years', mentioned in the following chapter, Jesus said, 'Your faith has healed you' (Matthew 9:22).

A few verses further on, we read of two blind men who followed Jesus, hoping to be healed. They replied in the affirmative to Jesus' question, 'Do you believe that I am able to do this?' whereupon 'Jesus touched their eyes and said, "According to your faith will it be done to you", and their sight was restored' (Matthew 9:29).

Again we read of extraordinary faith, that of a Canaanite woman who cried out to Jesus to heal her daughter (Matthew 15:22–28). We read that 'Jesus did not answer a word', as he 'was sent only to the lost sheep of Israel'. To his comment, 'It is not right to take the children's bread and toss it to their dogs', she replied, 'Even the dogs eat the crumbs that fall from their masters' table.'

Then we read that Jesus commended her faith: 'Woman, you have great faith!' he said, and he proceeded to heal her daughter.

HE IS ABLE

Let us come back just a moment to the healing of the boy with the evil spirit, related for us in Mark 9:17–25. Let's look at the way the father of the boy asks Jesus for help: 'If you can do anything, take pity on us and help us' (Mark 9:22).

'If you can…' He doesn't seem very sure, does he? Maybe he doubts whether Jesus can do anything.

Perhaps that is where you are in your praying. The situation has been going on for so long. There seems to be no change. Is Jesus really able to do anything about it? Well, can Jesus deliver or can't he? Can he give victory over sin or not? Can he give strength to do right?

Do you remember what Jesus replies to the father of the boy? 'Everything is possible for him who believes,' he says.

Then we have the affirmation of faith from the lips of the boy's father. And Jesus acts out of mercy and compassion, and according to the riches of his grace, and brings healing and deliverance to the boy. Towards the end of the account of this incident in Mark 9:28–29 we read: 'After Jesus had gone indoors, his disciples asked him privately, "Why couldn't we drive it out?" He replied: "This kind can come out only by prayer."'

Interestingly, in the parallel passage in Matthew's Gospel (17:20), Jesus is reported to have answered, 'Because you have so little faith.'

A REVOLUTION IN YOUR PRAYER LIFE

So we see the strong link between prayer and faith. If we put together these two answers that Jesus gave his disciples, as does William Lane in his *Commentary on the Gospel of Mark*, we could say that what they lack is a faith that prays 'a full reliance,' says Lane, 'upon the unlimited power of God expressed through prayer'.[10]

Do we, when we enter God's presence to seek his face, enter also into his will, into his purposes, as we spend time with him in prayer?

In concluding this look at 'Prayer and Faith', I leave you with one short verse, which you probably know; but do you believe it? If you do, it could revolutionize your prayer life. In the very next chapter of Mark, Jesus says, 'All things are possible with God' (10:27).

Do you believe that?

10

Spring Will Come

Hear my prayer, O Lord; let my cry for help come to you.

PSALM 102:1

WHEN GOD IS SILENT

'Isn't God supposed to make me happy?' asked Theresa, voicing a question which is perhaps at the back of many people's minds. Nowhere do the Scriptures imply that the Christian life is a bed of roses. Yes, the Bible talks of joy, peace, hope, and eternal life. All these are ours in Christ. But the Bible never hides the fact that Christians will suffer.

This book was initially going to be just a short series of devotional thoughts about prayer. Nothing complicated, nothing controversial. After all, we have many promises concerning answers to prayer in the Bible. 'Call upon me in the day of trouble; I will deliver you,' says God to his people (Psalm 50:15). 'Ask and it will be given to you,' says Jesus (Matthew 7:7). 'Whatever you ask for in prayer, believe that you have received it, and it shall be yours' (Mark 11:24), to quote just three.

But what about the times when God is silent, when he doesn't seem to respond to our prayers? What do we make of verses in the Bible like Job 13:24: 'Why do you hide your face...?' or Psalm 74:1: 'Why have you rejected us forever, O God?' And let us not forget that cry of anguish which escaped the lips of the Son of God himself, 'My God, my God, why have you forsaken me?' (Matthew 27:46b).

WE FEEL ABANDONED

Sometimes God seems far away. We cry out to him, but he does not seem to hear. We feel abandoned. 'Lord, take away the pain!' we shout. But the ache is still there, the sick feeling in the pit of the stomach.

If you feel like that, you are definitely not alone, and you are in good company! The psalms are full of such expressions of despair.

> *My heart is in anguish within me;*
> *the terrors of death assail me.*
> *Fear and trembling have beset me;*
> *horror has overwhelmed me.*
> PSALM 55:4–5

> *I cried out to God for help;*
> *I cried out to God to hear me.*
> *When I was in distress, I sought the Lord;*
> *at night I stretched out untiring hands*
> *and my soul refused to be comforted...*

Will the Lord reject forever?
Will he never show his favour again?
Has his unfailing love vanished forever?
Has his promise failed for all time?
Has God forgotten to be merciful?
Has he in anger withheld his compassion?

PSALM 77:1, 2, 7–9

How long, O Lord?
Will you hide yourself forever?

PSALM 89:46a

Hear my prayer, O Lord;
let my cry for help come to you.
Do not hide your face from me
when I am in distress.
Turn your ear to me;
when I call, answer me quickly.

PSALM 102:1–2

The psalmists pour out all their despairing feelings to God—their revolt, anguish and distress. We need to do the same.

TRUSTING GOD

Can we in all honesty ignore such cries from the heart? Can we skip over difficulties like these?

We may not have all the answers, but maybe we can at least give some thought to these problems. As we do, hopefully our eyes will be opened to discover a God who is far bigger than we had imagined, an infinite God who cannot be contained within the limits of human understanding, who cannot be boxed in, and who can show us the way.

'As the heavens are higher than the earth, so are my ways higher than your ways and my thoughts than your thoughts,' says God (Isaiah 55:9). This almighty God came down to our level in the person of Jesus Christ, and he wants to have a relationship with us. He wants us to trust him. He wants us to pray to him, to seek his face. Because he is able!

What do we mean exactly when we talk about having faith? Do we mean that God will do everything we ask him to do and give us everything we want? Or do we mean that we submit to him and trust him to work out his purposes in accordance with his perfect will?

How do we feel and what do we think when God doesn't answer our prayers? We may have prayed for healing for someone who is sick, and that person has died. Did God not hear our prayers? Why did he not grant our request?

These are questions we cannot always answer. How can our finite minds possibly understand the ways of an infinite God? But let us not forget that this almighty God is also our heavenly Father, who loves us and wants the best for us.

Will we trust him? Difficulties can either draw us closer to God, as we wrestle with the problems, or cause us to harden our hearts in unbelief.

Do you sometimes feel, when you are wrestling in prayer, that you need to 'pray a situation through', that is to say, pray on until God answers? Perhaps there are times when we need to do this. It was certainly the experience of Jacob, who told the Lord in no uncertain terms, 'I will not let you go until you bless me' (Genesis 32:26).

At other times, we will just lay a disturbing problem before the Lord, as King Hezekiah did with a crucial letter: 'Hezekiah received the letter from the messengers and read it. Then he went up to the temple of the Lord and spread it out before the Lord' (2 Kings 19:14).

Having done that, we too will leave the matter with God and trust him to work in his way and in his time.

THE UNFOLDING OF THE SEASONS

But how impatient we get sometimes! Why doesn't God provide instant answers? Sometimes he does, and we can praise him for that. Often he doesn't. Can we praise him then, too?

We want to see situations changed because of our prayers. We want to see lives transformed. It would seem that God's transforming work is usually progressive—a process, often long. Take the unfolding of the seasons, for example. It takes a long time for the sleep of winter to give way to the new life of spring, and even longer for the fruit on the trees to ripen and come to maturity.

God works in the same way in our lives and in the lives of those for whom we pray and the situations we bring before him. Winter seems very long and bleak at times. But spring will come!

GOD WILL NEVER FORSAKE US

When we are injured or incapacitated, we often feel alienated from God. We must not believe that feeling. God has promised that he will never abandon us: 'Never will I leave you; never will I forsake you' (Hebrews 13:5).

One thing we can always count on is his presence with us. When that terrible cry, 'My God, my God, why have you forsaken me?' escaped the lips of Jesus, it was because he was bearing our sin—yours and mine—on the cross, so that never again would we be separated from our heavenly Father.

We read in Paul's letter to the Romans that nothing can separate us from God's love:

I am convinced that neither death nor life,
neither angels nor demons,
neither the present nor the future,
nor any powers,
neither height nor depth,
nor anything else in all creation,
will be able to separate us from the love of God
that is in Christ Jesus our Lord.
ROMANS 8:38–39

So many passages of Scripture deal with suffering in one way or another. We are exhorted to rejoice in our trials because we know that the outcome will be faith, refined and strengthened.

'Consider it pure joy, my brothers, whenever you face trials of many kinds, because you know that the testing of your faith develops perseverance,' writes James (1:2–3).

The apostle Peter adds, 'You may have had to suffer grief in all kinds of trials. These have come so that your faith—of greater worth than gold, which perishes even though refined by fire —may be proved genuine and may result in praise, glory and honour when Jesus Christ is revealed' (1 Peter 1:6–7).

When we are called upon to suffer because of our faith, it means we share in the sufferings of Christ. For that reason, we can take heart, as Peter tells us. 'Do not be surprised at the painful trial you are suffering… But rejoice that you participate in the sufferings of Christ' (1 Peter 4:12–13).

We can also look beyond this world to that 'eternal glory' which our present afflictions are achieving for us: 'Our light and momentary troubles are achieving for us an eternal glory that far outweighs them all' (2 Corinthians 4:17).

Our troubles here and now, which may be severe and ongoing, are only qualified as 'light and moment-ary' as they are compared and contrasted with the 'eternal glory'. Paul exclaims in his letter to the Romans, 'I consider that our present sufferings are not worth comparing with the glory that will be revealed in us' (Romans 8:18).

Similarly, the writer of the letter to the Hebrews tells us that Jesus endured the pain and the shame of the cross for the 'joy set before him' (Hebrews 12:2).

Knowing that there is a purpose in our suffering can give us the courage to go on. John White, in his book *The Cost of Commitment*, thanks God:

...that he can turn the suffering to serve his own purposes in my life. I thank him that because Jesus as man suffered more than I ever will, God understands how I feel from personal experience. And as I praise and thank him, I become aware of two things. The suffering lessens. It lessens because the anxiety and fear that accompanied it have gone. (Peace in suffering halves its intensity.) In addition, hope is born as well as a sense of meaning in the suffering. I become almost excited that it will turn to my good. No longer do I wonder how I will bear the suffering. Suffering becomes a sort of chariot on which I ride to new planes of living.[11]

We will give the last word to the apostle Paul, who writes, 'To keep me from being conceited... there was given me a thorn in the flesh, a messenger of Satan, to torment me' (2 Corinthians 12:7).

Who gave him this 'thorn'? He refers to it as a 'messenger of Satan'. Satan's purposes are always destructive: it was given in order to torment him.

And yet, Paul gives a positive reason too for this 'thorn in the flesh'. It was to prevent him from becoming conceited. (This may have been a special snare ahead of Paul, as we know that he was highly intelligent, among the most well-educated of his day and full of leadership abilities from God.) His suffering served, from Paul's perspective, a good, constructive purpose, originating surely in God. We can only conclude then that what Satan purposed for evil, God turned around and transformed into good.

GOD'S GRACE IS SUFFICIENT

God's answer to Paul's repeated prayer for deliverance from his suffering, before he reached acceptance of it, was, quite simply, 'My grace is sufficient for you, for my power is made perfect in weakness' (2 Corinthians 12:9).

If God's grace was sufficient for Paul, it is also sufficient for you today. His power is still 'made perfect in weakness'. Paul understood this, and it led him to utter that confident cry of victory and triumph: 'I will boast all the more gladly about my weaknesses, so that Christ's power will rest on me. That is why, for Christ's sake, I delight in weaknesses, in insults, in hardships, in persecutions, in difficulties. For when I am weak, then I am strong' (2 Corinthians 12:9–10).

This same strength is available to you in your weakness. Can you echo these triumphant, victorious, confident, glorious words of the apostle Paul? Is this same experience yours? If not, it can be!

11

Tossed by the Wind

Search me, O God, and know my heart…

PSALM 139:23

REASONS FOR UNANSWERED PRAYER

Scripture does give us some reasons, however, for unanswered prayer. 'If I had cherished sin in my heart, the Lord would not have listened,' exclaims the psalmist (Psalm 66:18).

But, if we seek his face and repent, the Lord is always ready to forgive. 'If we confess our sins, he is faithful and just and will forgive us our sins and purify us from all unrighteousness,' writes the apostle John (1 John 1:9).

The apostle James attributes unanswered prayer to lack of faith on the part of the one who asks. He writes:

If any of you lacks wisdom, he should ask God, who gives generously to all without finding fault, and it will be given to him. But when he asks, he must believe and not doubt, because he who doubts is like a wave of the sea, blown and tossed by the wind. That man should not think he will

receive anything from the Lord; he is a double-minded man,
unstable in all he does.

JAMES 1:5–8

For God to answer your prayers, you must ask with
pure motives. James also says, 'When you ask, you do
not receive, because you ask with wrong motives, that
you may spend what you get on your pleasures' (James
4:3). In other versions, this word 'pleasures' is trans-
lated 'lusts'.

We have the sober example of Esau (recorded for us
in the book of Genesis) who forfeited God's blessing
and approval because of a desire for instant gratification. Returning home famished 'from the open
country' to find a tantalizing aroma wafting from the
kitchen, where his younger brother, Jacob, was
cooking lentil stew, Esau sold his birthright (a privilege
belonging to him as the firstborn son, and carrying
with it a double portion of the paternal inheritance), in
order to satisfy his appetite. We can read the whole sad
account in Genesis 25:29–34.

'MOST BLATANTLY SELF-CENTRED PRAYER'

Another example of this wrong way of praying or,
rather, of praying with wrong motives, is given for us
in Mark's Gospel. We can be grateful for the words of
Jesus which serve to rectify our attitude as we come
before him in prayer or as we interact with our fellow
believers: 'Whoever wants to become great among

you must be your servant,' he said (Mark 10:43). This teaching is in response to a rather strange request by James and John: 'Teacher,' they said, 'we want you to do for us whatever we ask' (Mark 10:35).

John Stott qualifies this statement as 'the worst, most blatantly self-centred prayer ever prayed'.[12] We know from the text that what they went on to ask for was basically selfish and reveals a greed for power and honour. 'Let one of us sit at your right and the other at your left in your glory' was the substance of their prayer. We need to come before the Lord in humility, conscious of our own unworthiness.

SERVANTS

Jesus gave us a living example of his teaching on servanthood when he washed his disciples' feet, as related for us in John 13: 'He got up from the meal, took off his outer clothing, and wrapped a towel round his waist. After that he poured water into a basin and began to wash his disciples' feet, drying them with the towel that was wrapped round him' (vv. 4–5).

When he had finished, he asked them, 'Do you understand what I have done for you?' (v. 12).

And he concluded, 'Now that I, your Lord and Teacher, have washed your feet, you also should wash one another's feet. I have set you an example...' (v. 15).

No room here for the kind of prayer uttered by James and John!

Why not search our hearts before God, and see what sin is lingering there? Are our prayers basically selfish? Are we greedy for power and honour and respect and prestige? What are our motives in coming before the Lord in prayer? Are we lacking in faith? Let us come to him for cleansing right now, by praying the concluding words of Psalm 139.

> *Search me, O God, and know my heart;*
> *test me and know my anxious thoughts.*
> *See if there is any offensive way in me,*
> *and lead me in the way everlasting.*
>
> PSALM 139:23–24

12

For His Name's Sake

Some of my reflections on prayer started out as a series of Bible reading notes I was asked to write. I have been sharing with you some of the experiences the Lord took me through while I was writing those notes about prayer.

It did not all stop there, as you can well imagine. God continues to speak, to teach, to show the way. The writing of the notes was not all smooth sailing. From time to time I got bogged down, but at such times the Lord used different people to encourage me and spur me on.

GETTING 'UNSTUCK'

I remember feeling particularly 'stuck' one Wednesday evening. I went as usual to our church prayer meeting, where we had an unexpected visit from some former members of our church now living in Florida.

As they came into the room, they put a beautifully wrapped present into my hands. I unwrapped it immediately and pulled out a book. Imagine my de-light when I discovered that it was a book on prayer—*Prayer, the Great Adventure* by David Jeremiah.[13]

I opened it at the Introduction, where the very first

sentence included quotes from a book that was lying right then on my desk at home: *With Christ in the School of Prayer* by Andrew Murray.[14] That unexpected present came to me as a great stimulus to get on with writing my notes.

Eventually, I finished the notes on prayer and sent them off for publication.[15] Shortly after, a friend of mine in France, where I live, became seriously ill and was unable to travel to England to attend a conference. She asked me if I would like to replace her. I agreed, even though I was completely ignorant of the subject of the conference.

Not long before I left home I discovered that the theme was 'Do we really know how to pray?' It was an excellent conference, with good teaching on prayer as well as opportunities to pray with others. I was much encouraged by the teaching and fellowship with Christians from different countries.

ANOTHER ROUGH SPOT

Back home after the conference, I resumed my usual routine. Some time later, I hit another rough spot. And I found myself going through a time of re-examination and inner turmoil.

I spoke to a friend about it and said, 'I don't even know how to pray any more.' Then I added, 'And I've just come back from a conference on prayer!'

'Yes,' he said. 'And you've just written a series of notes on the subject!'

So I had! In fact, I had finished my notes on prayer, read the book I was given (and many more besides), attended the conference on prayer; but for some reason all I could do at that point was echo the words of the psalmist who cried out, 'I am too distressed even to pray' (Psalm 77:4, LB).

The struggle continued, and my friend said to me one day, 'Why don't you take another stroll through Psalm 23, and I'll follow you with my prayers.'

'FOR HIS NAME'S SAKE'

And so began another stage in this 'great adventure' in prayer. After an initial rereading of the psalm, I wrote in my journal:

Bruised and battered, I came before the Lord this morning. What stood out to me in Psalm 23 was the phrase 'for his name's sake' (v. 3), which raises the question 'Why do I pray?' Prayer, that simple dialogue between father and child, suddenly seems very complex. I keep screaming out to God, 'I don't know how to pray!'

Psalm 23 had often been a lifeline to me in times of trouble. Reciting it slowly and meditatively during sleepless stretches of the night had restored peace and calm to my agitated soul and given me the longed-for rest.

This time, however, before making 'me lie down in green pastures', the Shepherd took me along a different track.

I sat up, alert, as I read, 'He guides me in paths of righteousness for his name's sake.' That little phrase, 'for his name's sake', caused me to stop and think. First of all, what does it mean? And then, if it is 'for his name's sake' that he 'guides me in paths of righteousness', maybe everything else he does is 'for his name's sake' as well? So, perhaps that should be my focus too?

THE SIGNIFICANCE OF A NAME

'For his name's sake'—one of those phrases we almost take for granted. Four words we read or hear from time to time, tacked on to one statement or another, without even thinking about the meaning of them.

We know that the Scriptures attach much more importance to a name than we do in Western Europe or the United States, though some countries and cultures of the world do still choose for their children names weighty with meaning. Names in the Bible, however, go even further, being expressions of the very character and nature of those who own them. The name is in fact the equivalent of the person.

So in that short, seemingly insignificant phrase, 'for his name's sake', we see that God's character, and therefore his reputation, is at stake. There is great meaning there!

And if he leads us in 'paths of righteousness' or 'right paths', it is so that his name will be vindicated. What we *do* and *are* reflects on God. If we profess to be his children, the sheep belonging to the Shepherd (staying with the imagery of Psalm 23), then what we do and the way we behave is not just our own business (as we may sometimes, mistakenly, think it is— autonomous, independent creatures that we tend to want to be). No, our conduct is a reflection on the Shepherd we profess to follow.

'He guides us in paths of righteousness for his name's sake.' The way we walk—if we follow God's leading along the right paths—will reflect on him and bring him honour. Conversely, if we choose to take wrong paths, we will bring shame upon him—upon his name, his character, his person.

A BIGGER PERSPECTIVE

God had much to say about his name in the instructions he gave to his prophet Ezekiel, and this helps us to understand the reference in Psalm 23. In Ezekiel 36:22–23, God said:

...say to the house of Israel, 'This is what the Sovereign Lord says: It is not for your sake, O house of Israel, that I am going to do these things, but for the sake of my holy name... Then the nations will know that I am the Lord...'

He then proceeded to tell Ezekiel exactly what blessings he was going to pour out upon his people, and he said again:

'I want you to know that I am not doing this for your sake... Then the nations around you that remain will know that I the Lord have rebuilt what was destroyed and have replanted what was desolate... Then they will know that I am the Lord.'

EZEKIEL 36:32, 36, 38

It was 'for his name's sake'.

'He guides me in paths of righteousness' not primarily for my own good, my own comfort, my own protection, though these are all by-products of his leading, but rather 'for his name's sake'.

Similarly, all he gave to his people—the redemption, cleansing, forgiveness, salvation, as well as the material blessings such as food and houses, recorded for us in Ezekiel 36—was not primarily for their own advantage, even though they benefited greatly, but 'for the sake of [his] holy name'.

Psalm 106:8 gives us perhaps a clearer understanding of this. We read that God saved his people 'for his name's sake, to make his mighty power known'. This gives us a much bigger perspective on life.

WHAT IS THE PURPOSE OF PRAYER?

The preoccupation with God's 'name' will also affect our praying. Why do I pray? What do I pray for? When I pray, is it 'for his name's sake' or for the sake of my own advancement and gratification? What is the aim of my praying—the glory of God, or the well-being of humankind?

As we have seen in the book of the prophet Ezekiel, the two often go together: God is glorified through what he does for his children, whom he greatly loves. But what is our focus? God's glory, or the fulfilment of our needs or, even worse, of our selfish desires?

When we look at the world at large, with all the conflict, terrorism, persecution, famine, and natural disasters, do we pray that God will intervene and act 'for his name's sake'—for his honour and glory? When we pray for missionaries in far-off lands, do we stop at their own comfort and well-being, or do we pray that God might be glorified through the blessings we ask him to shower upon them, so that he might be revealed to the surrounding nations.

GREEN PASTURES

My 'stroll through Psalm 23' was not the peaceful meander I expected it to be! Seeking refreshment and restoration for my own soul, I was pulled up short by an encounter with the Good Shepherd, the one who laid down his life for the sheep who listen to his voice and follow him (John 10:11, 27). My focus, which at that time was on myself and my problems, on my pain and weariness, changed dramatically as I began to ask myself questions about the bigger picture.

You can see a progression and a process that I had gone through, and not an easy one. At first, my thoughts had been in confusion. I felt I no longer knew how to pray. Then I was faced with my own selfishness. I was obliged to question my motives, to examine my desires, to search my heart. But soon, with the words of the apostle John ringing in my ears—'Your sins are forgiven you *for his name's sake*' (1 John 2:12, KJV, emphasis added)—I took courage and walked out of the dark valley and into the green pastures.

13

The Fullness of God

We often think of prayer as a private, personal occupation. And so it must be, of course. But not exclusively so, and not always. We certainly need to spend time alone with God in prayer. However, the Christian life is not meant to be lived out in isolation, but in fellowship with other believers.

In fact we have a very special promise from Jesus concerning our meeting together to pray: 'If two of you on earth agree about anything you ask for, it will be done for you by my Father in heaven. For where two or three come together in my name, there am I with them' (Matthew 18:19–20).

COMING TOGETHER TO PRAY

If you read through the book of Acts, you will find Christians praying together continually. 'They all joined constantly in prayer' (Acts 1:14). After Peter and John had appeared before the rulers, elders and teachers of the law, we read that they 'went back to their own people and reported all that the chief priests and elders had said to them. When they heard this, they raised their voices together in prayer to God' (Acts 4:23–24).

And in Acts 6 we read that one of the reasons the twelve apostles asked the disciples to choose seven men 'to wait on tables' was so that they themselves could give their 'attention to prayer' (Acts 6:4).

In Acts 4:23–30, we have an account of a prayer meeting in the early Church: 'Enable your servants to speak your word with great boldness. Stretch out your hand to heal and perform miraculous signs and wonders through the name of your holy servant Jesus.'

The prayer was answered, and we read in the very next verse that 'after they prayed, the place where they were meeting was shaken. And they were all filled with the Holy Spirit and spoke the word of God boldly.'

God wants us to be a part of the outworking of his purposes, and to this end we need to come before him for equipping and enabling.

We have a lovely example of a church at prayer in Acts 12:1–17. We read: 'Peter was kept in prison, but the church was earnestly praying to God for him' (v. 5).

These prayers were effective and God answered. 'Now I know without a doubt that the Lord sent his angel and rescued me,' realized Peter, when he eventually 'came to himself'.

We read that 'when this had dawned on him, he went to the house of Mary the mother of John, also called Mark, where many people had gathered and were praying' (Acts 12:12). When the door was eventually opened to him, due to his insistent knocking, the people within registered joy and astonishment.

Do you think they had really believed that God

would grant their request? Peter 'described how the Lord had brought him out of prison' (Acts 12:17). What a tremendous and clearly visible answer to prayer!

STRENGTHENED WITH POWER

Many of the apostle Paul's prayers for the early Church are recorded for us in his letters. In one letter, he tells the Christians in Ephesus:

I kneel before the Father, from whom his whole family in heaven and on earth derives its name. I pray that out of his glorious riches he may strengthen you with power through his Spirit in your inner being, so that Christ may dwell in your hearts through faith. And I pray that you, being rooted and established in love, may have power, together with all the saints, to grasp how wide and long and high and deep is the love of Christ, and to know this love that surpasses knowledge—that you may be filled to the measure of all the fullness of God.

EPHESIANS 3:14–19

What a prayer! It just makes me realize how petty and earthbound some of my own requests are, how small my vision. My finite mind cannot take in the dimensions of God's love or the extent of his purposes, and for that reason, I am sure that I must pray for lesser things than what he desires to give to his children.

What a comfort to be reminded of some other

words of Paul, in the very next verse of this same chapter, to the effect that God 'is able to do immeasurably more than all we ask or imagine' (Ephesians 3:20). In some way, through our imperfect praying and our limited vision, we can contribute to the fulfilment of his perfect plans and purposes.

HOW BIG IS YOUR VISION?

Let us look a little more closely at the four petitions that make up this prayer for the church in Ephesus. Why not echo these same requests as you pray for members of your own church? Paul prays:

* that they may be strengthened by the indwelling of Christ by the Spirit.
* that they may be rooted and grounded in love.
* that they may comprehend Christ's love in all its dimensions, although it surpasses knowledge.
* that they may be filled with all the fullness of God.

In the particular context of Paul's letter to the Ephesians, this love crosses deep racial and cultural barriers. It is not at all difficult for me to make an analogy with my own church in Geneva, Switzerland, composed of members from many different countries, cultures and races.

Paul prays that believers may know Christ's love in all its dimensions—width, length, height, and depth. Notice that it is 'with all the saints' (v. 18), and not in isolation, that Christians will have the power to grasp such a love, as it is expressed through their brothers and sisters in Christ.

Even then, having understood and experienced something of this love, we cannot fully comprehend it here on earth. And that brings us to Paul's final petition, that these Christians might be filled with 'all the fullness of God'. This too goes beyond the scope of life in this world, and can surely only be completely fulfilled in heaven. And yet, we should be growing into this 'fullness of God' even now. What a prayer, and what a program!

14

The Privilege of Prayer

And it is he who will supply all your needs from His riches in glory, because of what Christ Jesus has done for us.

PHILIPPIANS 4:19 (LB)

I hope that, after reading this book, you may have a greater awareness of the tremendous privilege we have in seeking God's face in prayer.

What a privilege, first of all, to be able to come before a holy, almighty, creator God, king of the universe, and have direct access into his presence through the blood of Christ, and call him 'Father'.

What a privilege to be able to adore him, praise him, worship him, thank him for who he is and for what he has done.

And what a privilege to be able to confess our sins to him, knowing that we can count on his mercy and forgiveness and cleansing.

What a privilege to be able to come before him with our needs, knowing that he will supply them and satisfy them 'according to his glorious riches in Christ Jesus' (Philippians 4:19) because he loves us and cares for us.

What a privilege to bring before him the needs of others, to intercede on their behalf.

What a privilege to be prayed for, to know that others are interceding for us.

What a privilege to be able to come at any time and know that God is listening and will hear our prayers.

What a privilege to come before him in silence and solitude and spend long moments in his presence in worship, praise and adoration, thanksgiving, confession, supplication and intercession, and just commune with him.

What a privilege to be able to come during the hustle and bustle, the noise and busyness of life, and cry out to him in that secret place.

What a privilege to pray with others, to encourage them and be encouraged, knowing that the Lord has promised to be present with us, to hear and answer our prayers.

What a privilege to carry everything to God in prayer.

Let us avail ourselves of this great privilege!

1   Spurgeon, C.H., *The Treasury of David*, Volume I, Associated Publishers and Authors, Inc., 1970.

2   Hengstenberg, E.W., *Commentary on the Psalms, Volume I*, T.&T. Clark, 1919, p. 459.

3   van Dooren, L.A.T., *Prayer: The Christian's Vital Breath*, The Latimer Publishing Company (n.d.).

4   Hybels, Bill, *Too Busy Not To Pray*, IVP, 5th edition, 1991.

5   Morgan, G. Campbell, *The Practice of Prayer*, Oliphants, new ed. (n.d.).

6   Kaiser, Kurt, 'Pass It On', Bud John Songs/EMI Christian Music Publishing.

7   Ferguson, Sinclair B., *Deserted by God?* The Banner of Truth Trust, 1993, pp. 166, 167.

8   Morris, Leon, *1 & 2 Thessalonians: An Introduction and Commentary*, The Tyndale Press, 5th ed., 1968, pp. 102, 103.

9   Brother Lawrence, *The Practice of the Presence of God*, Mowbray, new edition, 1977, pp. 3, 5, 18, 21, 31, 42, 47.

10   Lane, William L., *Commentary on the Gospel of Mark*, Eerdmans, 2nd ed., 1975, pp. 331–335.

11   White, John, *The Cost of Commitment*, IVP, 1976, p. 14.

12   Stott, John, *The Cross of Christ*, IVP, 2nd ed., 1986, p. 286.

13 Jeremiah, David, *Prayer: The Great Adventure*, Multnomah Inc., 1997.
14 Murray, Andrew, *With Christ in the School of Prayer*, Spire Books, 2nd ed., 1965.
15 Adamsbaum, Beryl, 'The Privilege of Prayer', *Day By Day With God* September–December 2001, ed. Mary Reid, BRF and Christina Press, pp. 11–18.

OTHER RECOMMENDED BOOKS

Appéré, Guy, *Dialogue with God*, Evangelical Press, 1979.

Griffith Thomas, W.H., *Genesis: A Devotional Commentary*, Eerdmans, 7th ed., 1971.

Hallesby, O., *Prayer*, IVP, 12th edition, 1968.

King, Guy H., *Prayer Secrets*, Marshall, Morgan & Scott, 1940.

Stott, John, *God's New Society*, IVP, 1979.

SCRIPTURE INDEX

Ch. 7: Boldness

Psalm 139:13
John 1:14
Philippians 2:5–8
Luke 2:7
Matthew 3:13–17
Mark 3:31–32
Matthew 13:55–56
Matthew 4:2
John 19:28
John 11:35
Matthew 8:24
Mark 3:14
Luke 10:38–42
Isaiah 53:3, 7
Psalm 103:14
Hebrews 2:17–18
Hebrews 4:14–16
Habakkuk 1:13
Psalm 24:3–4
Romans 6:23
2 Corinthians 5:21

Ch. 8: Take It to the Lord

Psalm 139:1–4, 13, 15
Romans 5:8
John 3:16
Jeremiah 31:3
Luke 1:78
Psalm 103:13
Isaiah 66:13
Romans 8:32
Philippians 4:19
Psalm 107:6, 13, 19, 28
Psalm 116:1, 6
Psalm 118:5
Psalm 120:1
Psalm 16:5
Psalm 142:4–5

Ch. 9: Prayer and Faith

2 Corinthians 5:7
Isaiah 42:3
Mark 9:24
Mark 9:19–27
Matthew 6:30
Matthew 14:30b–31
Mark 4:40
Matthew 13:58
Matthew 8:10
Matthew 9:19–27, 29
Matthew 15:22–28
Mark 9:17–25, 28–29
Matthew 17:20
Mark 10:27

Ch. 10: Spring Will Come

Psalm 50:15
Matthew 7:7
Mark 11:24
Job 13:24
Psalm 74:1
Matthew 27:46b
Psalm 55:4–5
Psalm 77:1–2, 7–9
Psalm 89:46a
Psalm 102:1–2
Isaiah 55:9
Genesis 32:26
2 Kings 19:14
Hebrews 13:5
Romans 8:38–39
James 1:2–3
1 Peter 1:6–7
1 Peter 4:12–13
2 Corinthians 4:17
Romans 8:18
Hebrews 12:2
2 Corinthians 12:7
2 Corinthians 12:9–10

Ch. 11: Tossed by the Wind

Psalm 66:18
1 John 1:9
James 1:5–8
James 4:3
Genesis 25:29–34
Mark 10:43
Mark 10:35
John 13:4–5, 12, 15
Psalm 139:23–24

Ch. 12: For His Name's Sake

Psalm 77:4
Psalm 23
Ezekiel 36:22–23
Ezekiel 36:32, 36, 38
Psalm 106:8
John 10:11, 27
1 John 2:12

Ch. 13: The Fullness of God

Matthew 18:19–20
Acts 1:14
Acts 4:23–24
Acts 6:4
Acts 4:23–30
Acts 12:1–17
Ephesians 3:14–20

Ch. 14: The Privilege of Prayer

Philippians 4:19

Bible reading notes for women

You may be interested to know that Beryl Adamsbaum is a regular contributor to *Day by Day with God*, a series of Bible reading notes written especially for women, by women, and published jointly by BRF and Christina Press. The team also includes Diana Archer, Fiona Barnard, Wendy Bray, Anne Coomes, Molly Dow, Rosemary Green, Margaret Killingray, Chris Leonard, Hilary McDowell, Elaine Pountney, Wendy Pritchard, Elizabeth Rundle, Jennifer Rees Larcombe, Alie Stibbe and Sandra Wheatley. The notes are edited by Catherine Butcher.

Day by Day with God provides daily notes, including a short printed Bible passage, which explains and applies God's word, written by women who have themselves found the Bible an invaluable guide and encouragement. Each day's reading ends with a suggested prayer or meditation.

To subscribe to *Day by Day with God*, please complete the form opposite and return it to BRF at the address shown.

Day by Day with God Subscriptions

☐ I would like to give a gift subscription (please complete both name and address sections below)

☐ I would like to take out a subscription myself (complete name and address details only once)

The completed coupon should be sent with appropriate payment to BRF. Alternatively, please write to us quoting your name, address, the subscription you would like for either yourself or a friend (with their name and address), the start date and credit card number, expiry date and signature if paying by credit card.

Gift subscription name _____

Gift subscription address _____

_____

_____ Postcode_____

Please send to the above for one year, beginning with the next January / May / September issue: (delete as applicable)

	UK	Surface	Air Mail
Day by Day with God	☐ £12.45	☐ £13.80	☐ £16.05
2-year subscription	☐ £21.90	N/A	N/A

Please complete the payment details below and send your coupon, with appropriate payment, to BRF, First Floor, Elsfield Hall, 15–17 Elsfield Way, Oxford OX2 8FG

Your name _____

Your address _____

_____

_____ Postcode_____

Total enclosed £ _____ (cheques should be made payable to 'BRF')
Payment by: cheque ☐ postal order ☐ Visa ☐ Mastercard ☐ Switch ☐

Card no. ☐☐☐☐☐☐☐☐☐☐☐☐☐☐☐☐☐☐☐☐☐

Card expiry date ☐☐☐☐   Issue number (Switch) ☐☐☐☐

Signature _____

(essential if paying by credit/Switch card)

NB: These notes are also available from Christian bookshops. BRF is a Registered Charity

☐ Please do not send me further information about BRF publications